WORKBOOK

FOR

❖

LEADERS
EAT LAST

❖

A Self Reflective Practical Guide To
Simon Sinek's Book

**Why Some Teams Pull
Together and Others Don't**

KARL LUCAS

This Workbook Belongs To:

o--------------------------------o

o--------------------------------o

o--------------------------------o

o--------------------------------o

o--------------------------------o

DISCLAIMER:

*This is an UNOFFICIAL workbook and
not the original book.
This is not an affiliate, authorized,
approved, or licensed by the subject's book
author or publisher.
This workbook is meant as a companion
guide to the original book.*

WELCOME NOTE

Congratulations on taking the initiative to further your leadership development! This workbook is intended to help you reflect, learn, and build your leadership skills intentionally. As you go through these pages, you'll discover the opportunity to examine your leadership techniques, celebrate accomplishments, and learn from setbacks.

How to Use this Workbook

Set the tone:
- Start each reflection session with a clean mind.
- Find a peaceful place, set aside some time, and prepare your favorite writing instruments.

Capture daily experiences:
- In the "Reflection on Leadership Journal, write about your daily leadership activities, areas for growth, and how they affect your team's morale and productivity.

Reflect on Impactful Moments:
- Explore the "Impactful Moments" area for good leadership experiences and insights from obstacles. Use these ideas to develop your leadership style.
- Track your progress towards long-term leadership objectives by recording new skills and knowledge in the "Personal Development" area.
- Use the "Future Actions" section to define specific strategies to improve your leadership effectiveness. This becomes your action plan for continual develop-

- ment.
- In the "Commitment" box, reconfirm your commitment to leadership development. This is a strong confirmation and reminder of your commitment.

Remember that this workbook is intended to help you improve both personally and professionally. There is no right or wrong way to utilize it; customize it to meet your requirements. Consistent reflection will provide important insights regarding your leadership path.

Here's to your continuing development and success as a leader!

Best regards.

KARL LUCAS

INTRODUCTION TO LEADERS EAT LAST WORKBOOK

Welcome on your leadership reflection journey! As you engage in this investigation of your leadership practices, we are inspired by Simon Sinek's deep insights presented in his book, "Leaders Eat Last." Sinek masterfully illustrates the core of effective leadership by delving into the mechanics of successful teams and the critical role leaders play in creating a healthy workplace culture.

In "Leaders Eat Last," Sinek highlights the necessity of developing a trusting culture, valuing team members' well-being, and creating an atmosphere in which people feel appreciated and supported. Sinek addresses the concept of authentic leadership via entertaining tales and persuasive examples, arguing that it is not about position or power, but about the willingness to prioritize others' needs.

As you go through this reflection workbook, think about the important principles from "Leaders Eat Last" to get a better understanding of what it takes to be an inspiring and empowering leader. Consider how you may apply these ideas to your everyday leadership activities to create a workplace that fosters a feeling of purpose, safety, and satisfaction.

Allow the lessons from "Leaders Eat Last" to guide you on your leadership path. This workbook is intended to sup supplement the teachings in the book by providing you with an organized place to think, create objectives, and take meaningful actions toward being the leader you wish to be.

PART 1

Our Need To Feel Safe

1. Protection from Above

2. Employees Are People Too

3. Belonging

4. Yeah, but . . .

SUMMARY OF CHAPTER 1

In the chapter, Drowley's readiness to put his life in danger for his fellow soldiers serves as an example of the need for empathy in leadership. It throws doubt on the conventional theory of motivation by emphasizing a culture of selflessness and service to the greater good. Rather than being motivated by outside benefits,

Drowley's actions were motivated by a deeper sense of dedication and the need to defend his team. The chapter also highlights empathy as the most valuable quality that enables people to behave bravely and selflessly even in non-military situations.

The chapter also suggests that civilian organizations may benefit from military teachings by fostering a culture of empathy and concern for one another, which can result in comparable levels of team cohesiveness and success in any setting.

The chapter emphasizes the need for empathy and a "circle of safety" in fostering success on both an individual and organizational level.

KEY LESSONS

*NOTE DOWN THE MOST IMPORTANT LESSONS
YOU LEARNED FROM THIS CHAPTER*

Describe an instance when you acted with empathy in a difficult circumstance. How did your reaction change as a result of knowing how others felt?

Consider a choice that carries some risk. How did you strike a compromise between possible hazards and your obligation to others?

Think back to a period when you tried to be noticed. What effect did it have on your definition of success, and how does it stack up against somebody like Johnny Bravo?

Evaluate the working environment you are in now. Does it promote a culture of giving and serving others? Even in non-life-threatening circumstances, how might empathy help create such a culture?

SUMMARY OF CHAPTER 2

The disparate experiences of Hayssen Sandiacre workers before and after Bob Chapman took control set the tone for the chapter. Previously, employees felt like parts of a machine, subject to rigid regulations and little autonomy. Subsequently, Chapman empowered staff members and treated them as unique people, establishing a culture of trust and respect.

Bob Chapman's methodology highlights these two qualities as important success factors. According to him, treating individuals with respect promotes teamwork and a feeling of belonging, which boosts productivity and the general well-being of the company.

The chapter describes the particular adjustments Chapman made, such as getting rid of pay phones and time clocks, letting employees roam about the office freely, and promoting employee participation. These modifications produced a more transparent and trustworthy atmosphere where workers felt appreciated and committed to the company's success.

The chapter makes the case that treating staff members properly improves both their personal and organizational effectiveness. Businesses with strong wo rk cultures, like Hayssen Sandiacre, often beat their rivals in terms of income, stability, and creativity.

According to Chapman, a leader's job is to safeguard their team members in the same way that parents do for their offspring. According to him, employers must care for and assist their staff members by giving them a secure and rewarding work environment.

KEY LESSONS

NOTE DOWN THE MOST IMPORTANT LESSONS YOU LEARNED FROM THIS CHAPTER

What effects did Bob Chapman's leadership style, especially his focus on trust and empathy, have on the Hayssen Sandiacre culture? What effects did these modifications have on workers' perceptions of the organization and their roles?

How did the elimination of bells, time clocks, and other conventional control devices affect the way the Hayssen Sandiacre workplace was changed? What impact did this change in leadership philosophy have on the trust and feeling of autonomy among the staff members?

Can you point out specific passages in the book that best illustrate the idea of treating workers like family? How did the company's performance and culture improve as a result of this family-oriented approach?

What can be learned from the example about how trust and empathy affect relationships between coworkers and the company as a whole in the tale of the worker going through a personal crisis and everyone coming together to help him?

SUMMARY OF CHAPTER 3

The book's third chapter emphasizes the value of having a sense of belonging and how to establish a "Circle of Safety" in organizations. It highlights the significance of empathy, a feeling of community, and shared values in fostering collaboration and trust as it details the transformation process of recruits in Marine Boot Camp. The story of the four oxen defending themselves against the lion from Aesop is used to illustrate the idea of the Circle of Safety.

The book highlights how crucial a robust Circle of Safety is for high-achieving teams because it enables members to concentrate on outside obstacles as a group. The Spartan example highlights that an organization's people work together, not simply its goods or services, to create strength.

The Circle of Safety is established and maintained in large part by leadership, who likens the act of granting someone access to an organization to adopt a kid. Everyone in the company should benefit from the Circle of Safety, not just a chosen few.

The practical advantages of a robust Circle of Safety, such as improved cooperation, trust, and creativity, are highlighted in the chapter's conclusion.

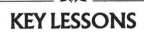

KEY LESSONS

NOTE DOWN THE MOST IMPORTANT LESSONS
YOU LEARNED FROM THIS CHAPTER

How can team leaders create and keep this circle in place? Consider how such a circle affects both individual and group performance.

Think back to an occasion when you were deeply a part of a group or organization. What particular elements led to this sensation, and how did it affect your performance and ability to work with others?

Think back to a time when you didn't feel secure or trusted in a group or organization. How did this impact your capacity to collaborate with others, speak clearly, and advance the objectives of the group?

Consider how the leadership in your present organization or previous experiences contributes to the creation of a feeling of community. What deeds or attitudes on the part of leaders helped foster a climate of collaboration, empathy, and trust?

SUMMARY OF CHAPTER 4

"Yeah, but..." Chapter 4 addresses the difficulties people have in finding happiness, contentment, and safety at work. It presents Ken, a middle-level executive at a global bank, who is dissatisfied with his position and doubts the utopian concept of working for an organization that concerns itself with the welfare of its workers.

The author highlights the practical and financial barriers that prevent such principles from being implemented in the real world, while also acknowledging the challenges leaders confront in fostering an atmosphere at work where people come before profit.

The chapter also addresses how job discontent affects one's mental and physical health, citing research suggesting that working at a job one despises is just as bad for one's health as being unemployed. The notion of "executive stress syndrome" is presented, casting doubt on the notion that jobs with more authority entail greater levels of stress. According to the British Whitehall Studies, feeling uncomfortable at work goes against natural inclinations and causes stress and subpar job output. It also shows a link between an employee's sense of control and stress levels.

The need for companies to establish "Circles of Safety" where workers feel safe is emphasized in the chapter's conclusion, which also makes the argument that this strategy is not just idealistic but also biologically based.

KEY LESSONS

NOTE DOWN THE MOST IMPORTANT LESSONS YOU LEARNED FROM THIS CHAPTER

Remember a period while juggling financial obligations and the urge for a rewarding career. How has this disagreement affected your well-being and level of work satisfaction?

Reflect on your experiences at work with autonomy and control, using the Whitehall Studies as a guide. What is the impact of control level on your work satisfaction and stress levels?

Think back to times when you decided to continue in a position despite its negative effects on your happiness and health because you believed it would provide work security

Have you worked somewhere where the welfare of the staff was given top priority by the leadership? What effect did this have on your work and the group dynamics as a whole?

ACTION EXERCISES

Program for Leadership Shadowing:
- Launch a program for leadership shadowing in which senior executives work side by side with staff members at various levels for a day.

Staff Narrative Sessions:
- Arrange for frequent gatherings when staff members exchange personal tales or experiences from their lives away from the workplace.
- Inspire leaders to become involved and tell their tales.

Identifying with Diversity and Inclusion seminars:
- Hold diversity and inclusion seminars where the importance of individual differences within the company is emphasized.
- To create a more inclusive workplace, ask outside experts or make use of internal resources to teach staff members about other cultures, experiences, and viewpoints.

Open Forum "Yeah, but..." Discussions:
- Create an ongoing open forum where staff members may express doubts, anxiety, or "Yeah, but..." moments.
- It is recommended that leaders engage in active listening, provide constructive feedback, and collaborate with staff members to resolve issues.

Leadership Goal-Setting Journal

My Vision & Values

My Short-Term Goals	My Long-Term Goals

My Written Commitment

Action Steps

Goal 1 | **Goal 2**

Progress

Final Notes & Reflection

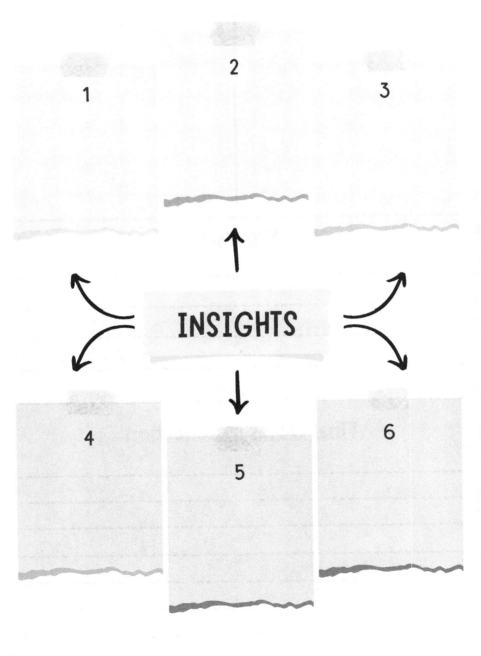

Leadership Vision Board

VISION 1

VISION 2

VISION 3

PART 2

Powerful
Forces

SUMMARY OF CHAPTER 5

The fifth chapter of "When Enough Was Enough" delves into the prehistoric environment of Homo sapiens 50,000 years ago, highlighting the difficult circumstances they encountered and the significance of collaboration in the early human journey.

It emphasizes how teamwork was the key to our ancestors' success. Endorphins, dopamine, serotonin, and oxytocin were natural rewards for actions that promoted both individual survival and group well-being.

The chapter also explores the paradox of humanity, highlighting the tension that exists between the interests of the individual and the group. It examines the moral conundrum that arises when people have to choose between their interests and the interests of the collective.

The chapter presents the idea of "selfless" chemicals, which promote social relationships, trust, and collaboration, and "selfish" chemicals, which are more concerned with individual objectives like tenacity and task accomplishment.

An essential aspect of the human experience, this dual

nature, which is divided between self-interest and the welfare of the community, shows how our biology developed to balance individual and social demands.

KEY LESSONS

NOTE DOWN THE MOST IMPORTANT LESSONS YOU LEARNED FROM THIS CHAPTER

How has overcoming obstacles been aided by your feeling of community and collaboration with others?

Consider how external job issues were handled. Did collaboration suffer from internal urgency?

Talk about instances when working together in a group had favorable results, in line with people's natural desire to cooperate.

When making decisions, how do you reconcile your objectives with the interests of the group?

SUMMARY OF CHAPTER 6

This chapter investigates how selfish chemicals affect human behavior and survival. It implies that because hunting and gathering provided a sense of accomplishment when we obtained necessities or accomplished our objectives, our ancestors employed endorphins and dopamine to promote these activities.

Dopamine, however, has a strong addictive potential and may result in negative behaviors such as drug addiction to substances including alcohol, nicotine, cocaine, and gambling. Serotonin and oxytocin, two social hormones that foster friendship and trust, are vital to human survival and development. Stress, contentment, and the desire to help others all decline when these substances are blocked, creating a vicious cycle of hostility and selfishness.

A feeling of responsibility and a drive to help others are created when oxytocin strengthens the relationships between parents, children, teachers, coaches, bosses, workers, and leaders. Serotonin plays a critical part in emotional and social elements of life, such as graduating from college. Oxytocin gives us a feeling of confidence and belonging by helping to channel our vulnerabilities.

KEY LESSONS

*NOTE DOWN THE MOST IMPORTANT LESSONS
YOU LEARNED FROM THIS CHAPTER*

How do dopamine and endorphins fuel our desire for success, and how have these neurotransmitters affected your goal-pursuing?

Think back to a time when you completed a task and experienced a dopamine rush. What effect did these substances have on your motivation and how did you see the accomplishment?

Examine your experiences creating trust using oxytocin. Can you think of a particular situation in which trust was essential, and what function did oxytocin play in that relationship?

Think about the role serotonin plays in promoting emotions of respect and pride. How has your feeling of achievement in both personal and professional settings been impacted by other people's recognition or approval?

SUMMARY OF CHAPTER 7

In Chapter 7, "The Big C," the influence of the stress hormone cortisol on human behavior in corporate contexts is explored. The chapter highlights how cortisol plays a key role in inducing the fight-or-flight response by drawing comparisons between the natural responses of a gazelle herd to possible dangers and human experiences in the workplace.

It looks at cortisol's physiological properties, its function as an early warning system, and how it relates to the body's fight-or-flight reaction. The story demonstrates how gossip and fears at work may cause a group of people to get stressed out, much like a gazelle seeing danger.

The chapter focuses on the negative consequences of extended exposure to cortisol, including weakened immune systems, heightened aggressiveness, raised blood pressure, and diminished cognitive performance. It makes the case that these detrimental impacts may be offset by a strong corporate culture marked by collaboration and trust.

The notion of a "Circle of Safety" is presented, emphasizing how crucial it is to feel comfortable at work to lower stress levels and achieve a positive work

work-life balance. A case study of Next Jump, a business that has a lifetime employment policy in place, is given to show how fostering loyalty and trust may boost revenue growth and lower employee attrition.

In conclusion, Chapter 7 promotes the development of a welcoming and encouraging work environment to lessen the negative consequences that long-term stress has on both people and businesses.

KEY LESSONS

NOTE DOWN THE MOST IMPORTANT LESSONS YOU LEARNED FROM THIS CHAPTER

Think back to a time when you experienced stress brought on by cortisol at work. What effects did it have on your performance and well-being?

Visit Next Jump to learn more about the idea of lifetime employment. In what ways does this policy strengthen the Circle of Safety and enhance worker performance?

Think about how cortisol affects trust and relationships at work. How do stress and a lack of collaboration among coworkers result from an inadequate Circle of Safety?

Talk about how serotonin and oxytocin contribute to a pleasant workplace atmosphere. How can managers give these substances top priority to improve worker satisfaction and overall productivity?

SUMMARY OF CHAPTER 8

The anthropological foundations of leadership and the reasons why leaders are innate in humans are examined in Chapter 8. The chapter explores the need for hierarchies to maintain order and collaboration by drawing comparisons between tribal behavior and contemporary companies. It presents the idea of alphas, or those who are seen as dominating, and describes how showing respect to alphas keeps a community in order.

The chapter places a strong emphasis on the value of leaders supporting their tribes and the reciprocal connection that exists between followers and leaders. It makes the case that serving and safeguarding the group is a duty of leadership, not only about personal benefits. The story investigates the effects of serotonin, the neurotransmitter linked to hierarchy and status, and how it shapes our actions inside social institutions.

The chapter emphasizes the social contract of leadership, which states that in return for their higher position, leaders are supposed to give security, using examples from society, including politicians and celebrities. It explores the negative outcomes when leaders break this pact, highlighting how crucial it is for leaders to put their tribes' welfare ahead of their in terests.

The premise that benefits and advantages are intended for the function one fills, not the person, is shown with a narrative about a former Under Secretary of Defense and a metaphor using a ceramic cup.

The story ends with the idea that strong and resilient communities are built by devoted and hardworking leaders who put their tribes' security and well-being first.

KEY LESSONS

NOTE DOWN THE MOST IMPORTANT LESSONS YOU LEARNED FROM THIS CHAPTER

What impact does the Chapter 8 discussion of the evolutionary need for hierarchical structures have on the dynamics of leadership in modern organizations?

Consider your opinions on the benefits and privileges that society bestows upon leaders. Do you think these advantages are warranted, or are there any areas that bother you?

Think about the story of the ceramic cup and the previous Under Secretary. In what ways does this story make you reconsider the nature of benefits and appreciation in the workplace?

Consider the Barry-Wehmiller case in light of the financial crisis of 2008. Have you ever taken or seen protective leadership actions that promote more allegiance and cooperation during trying moments in your professional life?

ACTION EXERCISES

Self-Reflection Time Capsule:
- Encourage team members to make a "Self-Reflection Time Capsule" in which they list their present objectives, difficulties, and sentiments on their job.
- Close the capsules and return to them at a certain time.

Opportunities for Every Day Service (E.D.S.O.):
- Establish an "Every Day Service Opportunity" program that runs on a weekly or monthly basis, encouraging team members to give a little bit of their time to help a colleague achieve a goal or project.

Workshop on "Courageous Conversations":
- Arrange a session on having "Courageous Conversations" at work. Give staff members the communication skills they need to handle challenging subjects, disputes, or problems.

Leadership Roundtable Conversations:
- Arrange for frequent roundtable conversations to be facilitated by various organization leaders.
- Every leader may discuss their motivations for taking on leadership roles as well as the difficulties they have encountered.

Leadership Reflection Journal

DATE: __/__/___

S M T W TH F S

Reflection on Leadership Practices

VALUES AND ARES OF IMPROVEMENT

Impactful Moments

POSITIVE LEADERSHIP MOMENT AND LESSONS LEARNED

Personal Development

NEW LEADERSHIP SKILLS OR KNOWLEDGE ACQUIRED

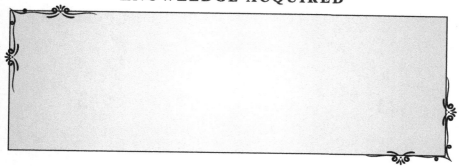

PROGRESS TOWARDS LONG-TERM LEADERSHIP GOALS

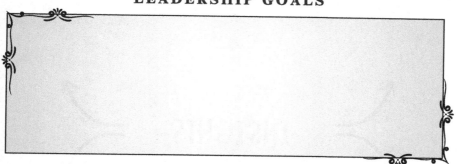

Future Action

----

6 Insights From This Section

1

2

3

INSIGHTS

4

5

6

PART 3

Reality

The incident of a Florida-bound aircraft when smoke entered the cockpit is told in Chapter 9, "The Courage to Do the Right Thing," which emphasizes the significance of knowing when to defy established norms.

The narrative emphasizes how companies can help their members develop a feeling of responsibility by providing them with training opportunities that extend beyond technical expertise to include judgment and decision-making skills. In this sense, trust is more than just abiding by the rules; it also means knowing when to break the rules for the sake of society as a whole.

The chapter highlights the need for mutual and shared trust between people and institutions, arguing that one-way trust is fundamentally broken. Building robust and durable organizational cultures requires this reciprocal trust.

The chapter also emphasizes how important it is for leaders to create an atmosphere in which people can be trusted to make the best choices, even when those choices go against the grain of society. The capacity for courage, or the will to behave morally, is fostered and strengthened by leaders who provide encourage-

encouragement and assurance from above, eventually fostering a culture in which people are encouraged to act morally in difficult circumstances.

KEY LESSONS

NOTE DOWN THE MOST IMPORTANT LESSONS YOU LEARNED FROM THIS CHAPTER

Consider the air traffic controller's choice to defy the emergency protocol. How does this highlight the value of trust in leadership, especially in terms of understanding when to break from the status quo?

Think about how trust functions inside companies. Why is reciprocal trust so important for a healthy and productive working relationship, and how does it affect the dynamics between leaders and their teams?

Consider whether you would put your faith in someone willing and able to breach the law when needed. In what ways does this viewpoint correspond with your notion of leadership trust?

Examine the notion that genuine trust can only exist between individuals—not in systems or regulations. What relevance does this idea have for your personal and professional experiences in various relationships?

In Chapter 10, "Snowmobile in the Desert," the paradox of human progress and the difficulties of living in a contemporary environment that unintentionally prevents collaboration are discussed. In his reflections on human intellect, the author notes that while the limbic brain plays a crucial role in regulating emotions, trust, and social relationships, our extraordinary accomplishments may be attributed to the neocortex.

The chapter makes the case that, despite our intellectual capacity, contemporary society has inadvertently produced circumstances that make collaboration more difficult. The search for happiness often appears elusive in affluent countries, where stress and feelings of isolation have given rise to prosperous self-help enterprises. The author talks about how the need for therapeutic services has paradoxically increased as the number of therapeutic professions has grown.

A snowmobile in the desert is used as an example to show how corporations often function in settings that are inappropriate for human collaboration. It is recommended that leaders understand that the problem is not with the individuals, but rather with the organizational environment. It is said that trust is like lubrication—it is necessary to minimize friction and improve performance. The chapter highlights that trust and commitment are difficult emotions to quantify or control because they have deep roots in the limbic system.

In the end, the chapter poses the issue of how society got into this figurative desert, inspiring readers to consider the surrounding circumstances that obstruct collaboration and confidence in contemporary institutions.

KEY LESSONS

NOTE DOWN THE MOST IMPORTANT LESSONS YOU LEARNED FROM THIS CHAPTER

How does collaboration in contemporary organizations be affected by the paradox of progress?

What can leaders do to meet the issues that today's organizational settings present? What can be learned from the snowmobile analogy?

*How does trust function as an
organizational lubricant, and how can
leaders concentrate on fostering trust?*

*What are the fundamental principles for developing
these feelings inside teams, and how can leaders
overcome the inherent challenges associated with
evaluating commitment and trust?*

ACTION EXERCISES

The Fortitude to Act Morally

- Consider a previous instance in which you had to make a moral or ethical decision at work. Jot down the solution and your approach to handling it. Think about other things you might have done.
- List a current situation at work when moral judgment is needed.
- Enumerate the possible outcomes of various acts. Seek advice from mentors or peers to obtain other viewpoints.

A snowmobile in a desert

- Review the objectives and tactics your business is currently using. Evaluate whether they are in line with the current state of affairs in your market and sector. Make a list of the changes that are required.
- Examine the market to identify new trends and possible disruptions.
- Make a suggestion and have a conversation with your group on how your company can successfully handle these changes.

Leadership Goal-Setting Journal

My Vision & Values

My Short-Term Goals	My Long-Term Goals

My Written Commitment

Action Steps

Goal 1	Goal 2

Progress

Final Notes & Reflection

----

6 Insights From This Section

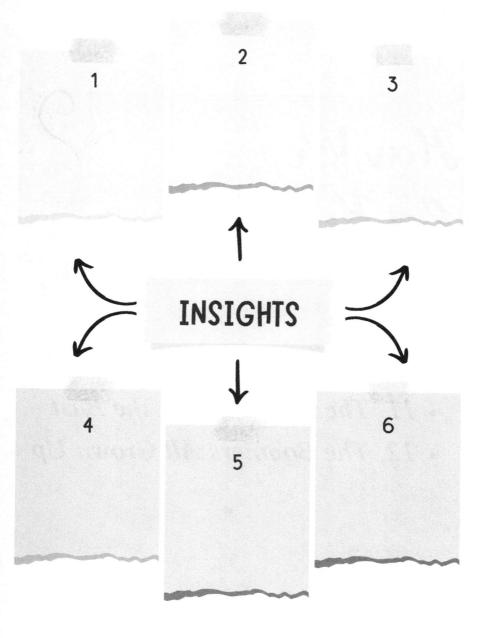

1

2

3

INSIGHTS

4

5

6

PART 4

How We Got Here

SUMMARY OF CHAPTER 11

The post-World War II period is examined in Chapter 11, "The Boom Before the Bust," with particular attention to the growth of the Baby Boomer generation and its effects on American culture. The wealth of the 1920s and the extraordinary post-World War II expansion and affluence known as the Baby Boom are both highlighted in this chapter.

Due to the Baby Boomers' upbringing during periods of increasing affluence and prosperity, the generation that placed a higher priority on individuality and self-realization than on service to others has changed.

After that, the story discusses how the Boomers rejected their parents' focus on hard labor and financial prosperity, leading to cultural shifts and rebellious attitudes in the 1960s. But when the Baby Boomers started working in the 1970s, they brought with them cynicism and self-centeredness that made them more individualistic and focused on protecting their riches.

The Boomers' rise to powerful positions in industry, government, and politics is covered in the chapter's conclusion, which also highlights the erosion of civility and bipartisanship.

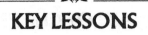

KEY LESSONS

*NOTE DOWN THE MOST IMPORTANT LESSONS
YOU LEARNED FROM THIS CHAPTER*

What role did the Great Depression play in the 1920s economic boom and how did it affect the thinking of the next generation?

What did the Greatest Generation mean when they spoke of duty and sacrifice, and how did World War II affect their moral compass?

What differences in attitudes and goals did the Baby Boom generation have from their parents, and how did their sheer numbers affect society?

When the Baby Boomers started working, what attitudes and behaviors changed, and how did these alterations affect the late 20th-century social, political, and economic dynamics?

SUMMARY OF CHAPTER 12

The book dives into the 1980s, a time of economic prosperity during which new ideas to safeguard Baby Boomer riches arose, in Chapter 12. Individualism was bolstered by the emergence of personal computers and other new technology, as well as by the rising acceptance of disposable goods and, regrettably, the idea that humans are expendable.

The chapter focuses on a crucial occasion that occurred on August 5, 1981: President Ronald Reagan dismissed more than 11,000 striking air traffic controllers, therefore creating a precedent for widespread layoffs. This incident signaled a change in corporate culture where safeguarding business was prioritized before human rights. Layoffs as a means of mitigating temporary economic shocks increased in frequency, hence changing organizational social norms.

We examine how putting business before people may lead to imbalances in corporate cultures and have an impact on huge companies. The chapter highlights the risks associated with such imbalances by linking this change to three notable stock market disasters.

The book promotes a return to leadership principles -

that place a higher priority on people than on money and highlights the need to reverse this mismatch.

KEY LESSONS

NOTE DOWN THE MOST IMPORTANT LESSONS YOU LEARNED FROM THIS CHAPTER

How do observations about the effects of individualism on society—as seen by the rise of personal computers and throwaway goods—follow from the technical revolutions of the 1980s?

Consider the effects of the massive layoffs that President Reagan ordered in 1981. What influence does this historical occurrence have on your perception of the goals of leadership and how they affect employees?

Given the consequences of putting business before people in the dismissals of air traffic controllers, how might people think about striking a balance between business objectives and worker welfare at work?

Examine one's own beliefs on abundance's abstract character in the modern world. What effects does abundance have on personal relationships, values, and self- and other perceptions in a society where resources are abundant?

ACTION EXERCISES

The Precursor Boom and Bust

- Look for past instances of businesses or sectors that had booms and then busts.
- Extrapolate lessons learned and see how comparable patterns may be identified in the current environment.
- Look for places in your business where development may not be sustainable.
- Create backup plans and approaches to reduce risk.

The Boomers Have All Aged Out

- Assess the leadership philosophies used in your company.
- Examine whether they are adjusting to the evolving demands of the contemporary labor force.
- To bridge the age divide, think about implementing mentoring programs.
- Have conversations with staff members of various age groups.
- Examine their viewpoints about leadership, work, and the future.
- Make use of this input to develop policies that encourage cooperation and inclusion.

Leadership Reflection Journal

DATE: __/__/___
S M T W TH F S

Reflection on Leadership Practices

VALUES AND ARES OF IMPROVEMENT

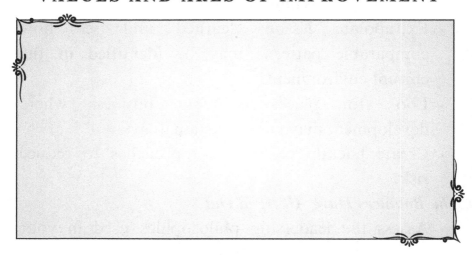

Impactful Moments

POSITIVE LEADERSHIP MOMENT AND LESSONS LEARNED

Personal Development

NEW LEADERSHIP SKILLS OR KNOWLEDGE ACQUIRED

PROGRESS TOWARDS LONG-TERM LEADERSHIP GOALS

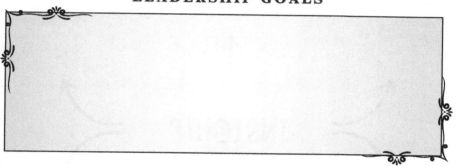

Future Action

----

6 Insights From This Section

1

2

3

INSIGHTS

4

5

6

PART 5

The Abstract Challenge

SUMMARY OF CHAPTER 13

The story opens in Chapter 13 with a startling scene in which a person is put through an electric shock experiment, emphasizing the power of authoritative figures to impose control and suppress empathy. The chapter then shifts to the period after World War II, emphasizing the Nuremberg Trials and the disappearance of several of the key players in the Holocaust's planning, including Adolf Eichmann.

The story focuses on Stanley Milgram's 1961 experiment, which was meant to investigate people's compliance with authority. To show that people are prepared to submit to authority even when it goes against their moral convictions, volunteers were given the task of shocking an actor who was one of the participants.

The experiment showed that even while the actor was distressed, a sizable percentage of individuals who were given authority continued to startle others.

Drawing comparisons between Milgram's experiment and modern corporate settings, the chapter highlights the dehumanizing effects of abstraction—in which people become disconnected from the results of their actions due to distance and numerical abstraction.

The story emphasizes how dehumanizing it may be to treat individuals like inanimate objects, akin to the consequences of authority-driven behavior shown in historical events and psychological research.

KEY LESSONS

NOTE DOWN THE MOST IMPORTANT LESSONS YOU LEARNED FROM THIS CHAPTER

Consider your deference to authority in ethically dubious circumstances, using the Milgram experiment as a guide. In what ways may this be relevant in daily life?

Examine how abstraction influences empathy and accountability in large-scale organizations, as shown by the Holocaust and Milgram's experiment. What effects does this distancing effect have?

Consider your personal responsibility beliefs in light of Milgram's experiment. In your life, how do you think there should be a balance between obeying authority and challenging it?

Think about the chapter's discussion of the wider effects of numerical abstraction in contemporary capitalism. How can it lead to possible cruel actions and contribute to dehumanization?

SUMMARY OF CHAPTER 14

In Chapter 14, the idea of abstraction in business is examined via a comparison of past occurrences and current methods. It draws attention to the 2009 salmonella epidemic and the consequences of weak organizational cultures in which workers defer to superiors.

The article also addresses the propensity to put financial objectives ahead of people's safety, using leaders like Stewart Parnell as instances of how this has happened. It refutes the idea that following the law is enough to ensure ethical conduct, citing examples of businesses taking advantage of legal gaps to their advantage.

The chapter also challenges the dominant belief that the only social duty of business is to maximize profits. Using the Titanic as a historical example, we can see the disastrous effects of following antiquated rules.

The last line of the text makes the argument that to avoid dehumanizing abstraction in decision-making, there must be a feeling of higher moral authority. Leaders who put people's needs ahead of numbers create an environment where people feel empowered to act morally even when doing so means making temporary sacrifices.

The chapter promotes a change in perspective from impersonal financial measurements to a more responsible and grounded method of making decisions.

KEY LESSONS

*NOTE DOWN THE MOST IMPORTANT LESSONS
YOU LEARNED FROM THIS CHAPTER*

Think back to a situation at work when people were not as important as measurements. Did that affect the dynamics of the team?

Consider times when moral obligation was subordinated to norms at work. What impact did it have on trust?

Think about making decisions using abstract notions. In what ways is the human effect taken into account?

Examine how morality or a higher authority figure in the process of making ethical decisions. How can leaders cultivate a feeling of accountability and purpose?

The Communist Party of the Soviet Union's General Secretary, Joseph Stalin, placed a strong emphasis on the value of genuine personal connection and the relationship between numbers and people. Because technology facilitates scalability and the dissemination of ideas but also makes relationships and communication more difficult, the virtual world has emerged as a major problem for businesses.

Shy individuals may speak out in online networks, but some are also free to behave in ways they probably wouldn't in real life. Face-to-face encounters have more significance for social creatures like us than virtual conferences or business travel.

Benefits from BlogWorld include exchanging ideas, meeting new people, uniting individuals, and getting to know others who share your interests. We feel a part of something, build trust, and have the ability to feel for others when we engage in real, live human connection.

A British anthropologist named Robin Dunbar, who teaches at Oxford University's Department of Experimental Psychology, has shown that humans are only able to sustain around 150 intimate connections. Since the advent of the Internet, it has become clear -

that communicating with a large number of people is not as effective as formerly believed.

Relying on hierarchies is the only viable option for bigger businesses to maintain the Circle of Safety while managing size. In the knowledge that their leaders would look out for them, managers must assume responsibility for the safety and well-being of individuals under their supervision.

KEY LESSONS

NOTE DOWN THE MOST IMPORTANT LESSONS
YOU LEARNED FROM THIS CHAPTER

In what ways do the accounts of the automobile accident and the Syrian crisis highlight the difficulty in relating to mass disasters as opposed to isolated incidents?

How does the value of in-person contacts connect to the shortcomings of the internet in terms of fostering meaningful, trustworthy relationships?

What effects does Dunbar's Number have on cooperation and leadership? Could you provide any personal instances of how a group's size affected its dynamics?

Examine the effects of donating time and effort vs cash in light of the accomplishments of the fund-raising division and the Wells Fargo Bank case study. What possible applications does this idea have for organizational leadership?

SUMMARY OF CHAPTER 16

In Chapter 16, the idea of imbalance is explored with particular attention to the problems that might occur when people or organizations possess an abundance of resources. It starts by talking about how, some 10,000 years ago, the economy changed from one of sustenance to one of excess, enabling commerce, population increase, and the rise of different classes.

The phrase "Destructive Abundance" is introduced in this chapter to characterize the outcomes of an unbalance between selfless and selfish goals, when the advancement of personal or organizational goals takes precedence over concerns for the welfare of society.

The biggest corporations often use lobbying to influence laws to their advantage by highlighting the dangers of pursuing corporate or personal goals without restraint. According to the author, Destructive Abundance is the product of improperly managed corporate cultures, when executives disregard their duties and put results ahead of protecting individuals who contribute to the imbalance.

The pattern seen in companies experiencing Destructive Abundance is highlighted in the chapter's conclusion, which also highlights the significance of honesty, effective leadership, and striking a balance between individual goals and group well-being.

KEY LESSONS

NOTE DOWN THE MOST IMPORTANT LESSONS YOU LEARNED FROM THIS CHAPTER

What effects has society's structure felt from the historical transition to surplus economies?

Consider situations when an excess of resources resulted in an imbalance. How was group dynamics affected by it?

How do you feel about "Destructive Abundance"?
Could you provide instances from businesses?

Examine how leaders might help avoid Destructive
Abundance. How important is striking a balance
between altruism and self-interest?

ACTION EXERCISES

Distraction Kills

- Point out instances inside your company where communication or procedures have been too abstract.
- Collaborate in groups to make these procedures more understandable and efficient by streamlining and clarifying them.
- Lead a discussion about the risks associated with abstraction.

Contemporary Abstraction

- Review the communication tools and technology stack in your company.
- Consider if they promote direct, unambiguous communication or whether they add to the deluge of information.
- Make changes to improve avenues of communication.
- Inspire team members to discuss how current abstraction has affected their job.

Controlling the Distraction

- Introduce frequent in-house training sessions on effective communication for staff members.
- Establish a feedback system that allows team members to confidentially voice issues with ambiguous or ethereal communication.

Leadership Goal-Setting Journal

My Vision & Values

My Short-Term Goals	My Long-Term Goals

My Written Commitment

Action Steps

Goal 1	Goal 2

Progress

Final Notes & Reflection

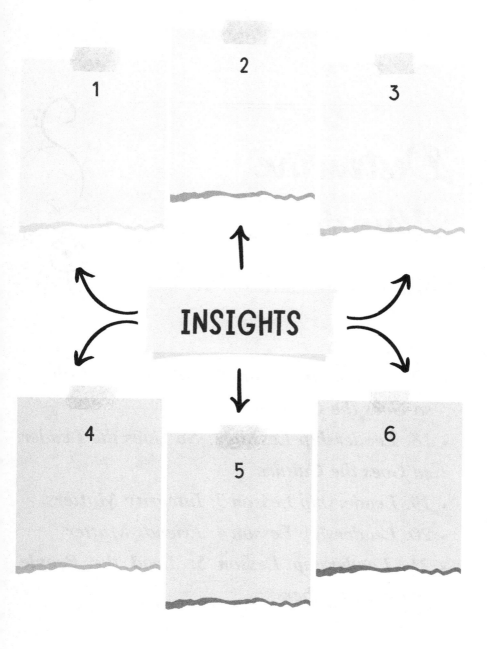

1

2

3

INSIGHTS

4

5

6

PART 6

Destructive Abundance

Chapter 17 uses case studies from Citigroup and Goldman Sachs to investigate the connection between leadership and company culture. Over time, the collaborative and trust-based "Long-term Greedy" mentality of Goldman Sachs gave way to a more aggressive and short-term-oriented culture. The 2010 mortgage-backed securities crisis further damaged its already damaged image.

The chapter places a major emphasis on the need to preserve a corporate culture that puts principles, honesty, and the welfare of employees ahead of profits in the near term.

Information hoarding was a result of Citigroup's poisonous culture, which made it more difficult for the company to handle the financial crisis. The culture deteriorated because of the leaders' attention to costs and income rather than the welfare of their workforce.

In contrast, 3M's positive culture places a strong emphasis on sharing and collaboration, which promotes creativity and worker wellbeing.

The chapter places a strong emphasis on how leadership affects corporate culture and how crucial a positive culture is to long-term success, placing a high priority on cooperation, values, and employee well-being.

KEY LESSONS

NOTE DOWN THE MOST IMPORTANT LESSONS YOU LEARNED FROM THIS CHAPTER

Consider Goldman Sachs' change in attitude from "long-term greedy" to more assertive. What impact has this move had on the company's image, and are there any similarities with other businesses?

Examine the notion that a business's culture serves as its "secret sauce." How does the loss of Goldman Sachs' cultural identity contrast with your own experiences at work? Which cultural components, in your opinion, are key to long-term success?

Compare and contrast the cultures of the Taj Mahal Palace Hotel and Goldman Sachs. In what ways do different cultures impact actions and choices, and what are the leadership takeaways for forging a robust company culture?

Examine how leadership affects culture by examining the tales of 3M, Citigroup, and Goldman Sachs. What roles have leaders played in shaping these cultures, and what potential differences in leadership styles could have produced?

SUMMARY OF CHAPTER 18

The link between corporate culture and leadership is covered in detail in Chapter 18. It opens with a warning about Stanley O'Neal, who changed Merrill Lynch's culture to one characterized by fierce rivalry and mistrust. O'Neal's obsession with power and self-interest brought to the company's demise.

The focus of the chapter then turns to US Navy submariner Captain David Marquet. Marquet, who had previously used a top-down strategy, found himself in a position where he had to adapt his management style.

He changed his paradigm from one that was leader-centric to one that gave the crew the freedom to think independently and assume accountability. The crew's level of trust, collaboration, and problem-solving improved as a result of this adjustment. Under Marquet's direction, the Santa Fe—once the lowest-rated crew in Navy history—rose to the top of the ratings.

The chapter highlights how crucial it is for leaders to cede control and give the best-informed people the authority to make choices.

The difference between Marquet's transformational approach and O'Neal's self-centered leadership emphasizes how different leadership philosophies affect company performance and culture.

KEY LESSONS

NOTE DOWN THE MOST IMPORTANT LESSONS YOU LEARNED FROM THIS CHAPTER

What effects did Stanley O'Neal's emphasis on personal aspiration have on the Merrill Lynch culture, and what effects may comparable leadership values have on your place of employment?

What are the most important lessons to be learned from Captain Marquet's transition to a culture of purpose aboard the USS Santa Fe, and how can you apply them to your own experiences leading others?

Consider Captain Marquet's discussion of leadership strength as the flow of energy. What effects does your organization's power structure have on how effective it is?

How did the deeds of leaders such as Saddam Hussein, Stanley O'Neal, and Captain Marquet affect confidence in their respective organizations? How have you personally seen choices made by leaders influencing trust in your career?

SUMMARY OF CHAPTER 19

Using examples from the business world and the Marine Corps, Chapter 19 explores the value of honesty in leadership. By telling the tale of a Marine candidate who slept off while on watch and first denied it, the author emphasizes how important it is to accept accountability for one's actions to foster trust.

The chapter highlights that as trust is the cornerstone of productive cooperation, honesty is essential in leadership. Using instances from the business sector, the author attacks dishonest executives and emphasizes how crucial honesty is to preserving confidence with both clients and staff.

A contemplation on how actions made by leaders affect trust and the need for honesty in all facets of leadership comes to a close in this chapter.

KEY LESSONS

NOTE DOWN THE MOST IMPORTANT LESSONS
YOU LEARNED FROM THIS CHAPTER

How does your approach to leadership and accountability compare or contrast with the Marine Corps' focus on character and direct responsibility?

Consider your approach to handling errors at the moment. How may your relationships and credibility be affected by an instantaneous commitment to accountability?

Think about the Bank of America example. What effect did the dishonesty have on the consumers' trust? Can you think of any situations when an organization's lack of openness made you less trusting of them?

Examine the "bedrock of trust" function that integrity plays in leadership. In what ways can leaders cultivate an environment of integrity, and what effects has integrity had on team dynamics in your own experiences?

SUMMARY OF CHAPTER 20

In Chapter 20, the significance of friendships and ties in politics is examined, with particular attention paid to how the composition of the US Congress has changed over time. It draws attention to a period when people from many political parties collaborated and became friends, highlighting the value of interpersonal relationships in promoting collaboration and trust.

The 1990s reforms, spearheaded by Newt Gingrich, are criticized in this chapter for elevating control over collaboration and creating a more polarizing political climate. The chapter makes the case that the present dearth of collaboration and trust in Congress is partly due to a lack of quality time spent together and a preference for fundraising over relationship-building.

The author illustrates how interpersonal relationships may transcend political divides and result in more efficient government with instances of bipartisan friendships, such as that between George McGovern and Bob Dole. Despite the difficult political environment, the chapter's conclusion makes the case that individual attempts to forge connections across party lines may promote more collaboration and advancement.

KEY LESSONS

NOTE DOWN THE MOST IMPORTANT LESSONS
YOU LEARNED FROM THIS CHAPTER

How does the chapter's description of Congress's transition from collaboration to competition relate to your own experiences in leadership or group dynamics?

Consider the items listed in the suggested itinerary for members of Congress. In what ways does this align or diverge from the priorities that you hold in your personal or professional life?

When considering the significance of time and effort dedication in establishing trust, how does this idea relate to your personal or professional settings?

Think back to situations in your life when you made unexpected friends and things worked out well. How could the tales of Representatives Goodlatte and Herseth Sandlin motivate you to take a different tack when it comes to partnerships or relationships?

SUMMARY OF CHAPTER 21

"Leaders Eat Last" addresses the idea of shareholder value and how it affects corporate leadership in Chapter 21. The chapter explores the historical trend of emphasizing shareholder value as a crucial indicator of business performance, particularly since the 1970s. It draws attention to how Milton Friedman's theories on profit maximization influenced people to prioritize short-term benefits above long-term stability.

A case study of Jack Welch, the former CEO of General Electric (GE), who gained notoriety for maximizing shareholder value by tying executive compensation to stock performance and implementing layoffs, is presented in this chapter. Though effective in the short run, the author contends that this strategy could not strengthen the business or leave a lasting impact.

The story compares and contrasts Welch's management approach with that of Costco co-founder James Sinegal, who placed a strong emphasis on fostering a people-first culture. The chapter makes the case that Sinegal's strategy, which prioritizes long-term organizational health and employee well-being, helped to sustain Costco's growth and profitability, particularly in lean times.

The author questions the idea that a company's main duty should be to maximize shareholder wealth, highlighting the need to have leaders who see profit as a tool for fostering a good organizational culture.

The assertion made in the chapter's conclusion is that a firm can only attain consumer loyalty and affection when its workers believe that its executives appreciate and care about them.

KEY LESSONS

NOTE DOWN THE MOST IMPORTANT LESSONS YOU LEARNED FROM THIS CHAPTER

What effects has the business culture's focus on shareholder value had on your career path and how does it affect your leadership style?

In your professional life, have you ever placed a higher priority on immediate results than long-term effects? If so, how did it affect your team's morale and the organizational culture?

*How can leaders foster a positive "Circle of Safety"
for their teams, and what effects does this have on the
well-being and productivity of the team?*

*Which mindset—people-first or profit-driven—do
you find yourself gravitating toward in your
leadership style? What effects does this strategy
have on morale, team loyalty, and overall success?*

ACTION EXERCISES

- Evaluate the culture within your company. Employ seminars, interviews, or surveys to get staff feedback on the current culture.
- Form a cross-functional group whose job it is to determine where cultural enhancements are needed. Make incremental, practical modifications that support the intended cultural transformation.
- To determine their own beliefs and leadership philosophies, leaders should evaluate themselves. Urge them to ask their teams for input so they can see how they are affecting the culture.
- Put in place leadership development initiatives that stress self-awareness and the role leaders play in influencing company culture.
- Create a code of conduct that prioritizes morality and honesty. Spread the word about this code and provide training sessions to make sure everyone understands it.
- Incorporate conversations on moral decision-making into group sessions. Using real-world examples, you may start discussions on how to be honest under pressure.
- Promote team-building exercises that help coworkers get along well with one another.

Leadership Reflection Journal

Reflection on Leadership Practices

VALUES AND ARES OF IMPROVEMENT

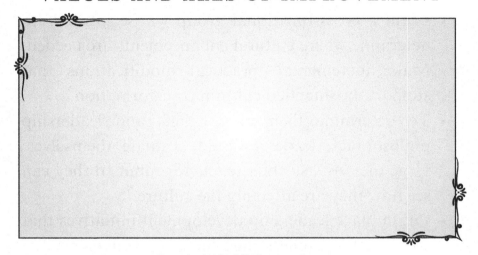

Impactful Moments

POSITIVE LEADERSHIP MOMENT AND LESSONS LEARNED

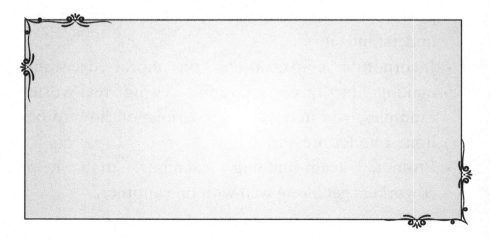

Personal Development

NEW LEADERSHIP SKILLS OR KNOWLEDGE ACQUIRED

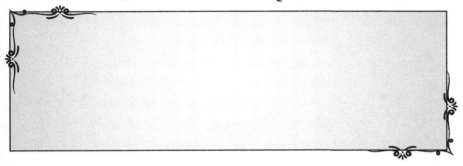

PROGRESS TOWARDS LONG-TERM LEADERSHIP GOALS

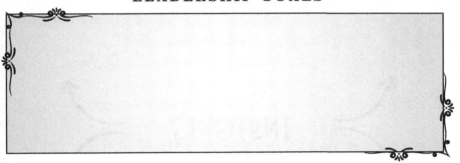

Future Action

1

2

3

INSIGHTS

4

5

6

PART 7

A Society Of Addicts

SUMMARY OF CHAPTER 22

The historical background of puerperal fever, an illness that struck women in the late 18th and early 19th centuries after giving birth, is examined in Chapter 22.

It draws attention to how physicians mishandled the illness throughout the Age of Enlightenment and neglected to take responsibility for their part in its growth. The pandemic began to wane only when Dr. Oliver Wendell Holmes identified the link between physicians and the disease's spread and the medical community adopted sterilization policies.

The chapter also stresses how important it is for managers to be accountable for the welfare of their workforce, stressing the risks of focusing just on efficiency goals and data without taking people's needs into account.

It also explores how addictive performance-driven societies can be, drawing comparisons between alcoholism and dopamine-fueled addiction to meeting corporate performance targets. The chapter ends with a call to action for managers: take on the role of a people leader, own up to their part in the issue, and prioritize employees' well-being inside the workplace.

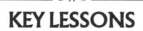

KEY LESSONS

NOTE DOWN THE MOST IMPORTANT LESSONS
YOU LEARNED FROM THIS CHAPTER

How could blind spots in today's corporate culture about employee well-being be related to the historical negligence of physicians in the Enlightenment era's puerperal fever outbreak?

Can you think of a circumstance at work when the significance of your team's well-being was subordinated to metrics? What were the ramifications, and how did it alter the dynamics of your company as a whole?

Consider whether any elements of your company's culture or leadership style inadvertently encourage a "dopamine addiction" in your staff. How can you prioritize your team's overall well-being by addressing this?

Given the chapter's emphasis on leaders safeguarding their people, what particular steps can you take in your position to make sure that your leadership is focused on your team members' well-being rather than simply numbers?

The effects of deregulatory policies on different businesses and the public interest are examined in Chapter 23. It draws attention to the benefits of restrictions in resource management, such as limiting emissions and oil drilling.

The chapter explores the historical background of broadcast sector rules, highlighting the FCC's responsibility for preserving a balance between private enterprise and public service.

The author emphasizes how the Iran hostage crisis caused network executives to get more involved and shift their goals, transforming journalism from a public service to a business. The Fairness Doctrine, which permitted news companies to embrace political viewpoints without offering balanced viewpoints, was repealed in 1987, and this is another topic covered in the chapter.

The chapter faults the media for underreporting and for overindulging in lighthearted but uninformative material, blaming these problems on the pursuit of profit over the common good.

The chapter also covers the fallout from the acts of the Baby Boomer generation, including how regulations in tended to curb excess and addiction have been undermined. Former CEOs apologize for their part in deregulating, and the author raises concerns about executives' lack of vision.

KEY LESSONS

NOTE DOWN THE MOST IMPORTANT LESSONS YOU LEARNED FROM THIS CHAPTER

What effects does the transition (covered in Chapter 23) from news as a public service to a profit-driven sector have on the goals and values of media companies?

Think back to a time in your life or career when pursuing financial success got in the way of moral principles or the welfare of society. What lessons may be learned from this event in light of the examination of profit-driven motivations in this chapter?

Think about situations in your setting when the repeal of laws like the Glass-Steagall Act and the Fairness Doctrine led to imbalances or unexpected effects.

How, in your opinion, can leaders strike a balance between their need to further the interests of society at large and their need for expansion and profit? Consider the difficulties mentioned in the chapter and make a connection between them and your own experiences or insights.

"The Abstract Generation" explores the social ramifications of generational changes in Chapter 24, with a particular emphasis on Generation Y. The author contends that the behaviors of past generations, especially the Baby Boomers, who protected their kids from adversity and created skewed ideals, are to blame for the present period of Destructive Abundance.

The story takes place against the background of the Boomers' early years of increasing prosperity and luxury as well as the growing cynicism that characterized the 1970s government. The Me Generation's belief that individual interests and riches should take precedence above social ideals was cemented over the ensuing boom years.

Along with contrasting the Boomers' willingness to work within the tax rules to the following generation's propensity to take advantage of every potential loophole, the chapter also looks at how views regarding work and commitment are changing.

The chapter also addresses the concerning rise in Baby Boomer suicide rates, as well as Generation Y's engagement with technology and its possible effects on behavior and attention spans.

KEY LESSONS

NOTE DOWN THE MOST IMPORTANT LESSONS YOU LEARNED FROM THIS CHAPTER

What attitudes and ideals have you developed as a result of your own parenting experiences? Consider the potential effects these factors may have on your choices and actions.

Think back to times in your life when you were impatient. What impact did it have on your relationships, decision-making, and personal development? What do you think you can learn from such encounters?

Consider how you feel about using technology and multitasking. What is your approach to handling distractions, and have you seen any changes in your capacity to concentrate and interact with others?

Examine your entitlement and impatience-related beliefs. How do these mindsets manifest themselves in your life? How may they affect the way you handle relationships, the workplace, and social issues?

ACTION EXERCISES

- Have an introspective discussion. Every person needs to pinpoint one habit or action that may be a factor in more serious societal issues. To promote candid conversation, feel free to share these views in confidence.
- Set up a conversation in your group on how individual decisions affect society's problems. Examine possible group initiatives to deal with these issues.
- Examine the company's social responsibility procedures and policies as they stand. Determine what needs to be improved, such as community involvement, fair labor practices, or environmental sustainability.
- Initiate a "Social Impact Challenge" at your company. Encourage staff members to suggest and carry out community or environmental improvement initiatives.
- Host seminars on information assessment and critical thinking. Give people the tools they need to evaluate and critically think about abstract ideas to promote an educated and conscientious society.
- Launch campaigns to raise awareness of the possible repercussions of accepting abstract concepts at face value. Promote frank discussion and fact-checking to counter false information.

Leadership Goal-Setting Journal

My Vision & Values

My Short-Term Goals

My Long-Term Goals

My Written Commitment

Action Steps

Goal 1	Goal 2

Progress

Final Notes & Reflection

----

6 Insights From This Section

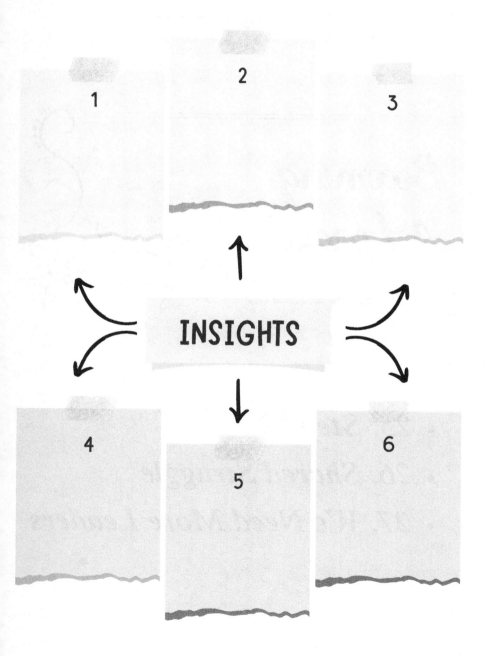

1

2

3

INSIGHTS

4

5

6

PART 8

Becoming A Leader

SUMMARY OF CHAPTER 25

In Chapter 25, "Step 12," the difficulties facing modern society are covered, with a focus on the internal risks that arise from inside organizations to human well-being. The author highlights the significance of recognizing systemic addiction as the first step by drawing comparisons between organizational addictions and the addictive nature of alcoholism. Step 12 establishes a Circle of Safety and highlights the value of sincere human connections in the healing process.

The chapter also explores how oxytocin and serotonin help people overcome addiction. Step Twelve essentials like selflessness, sacrifice, and service might cause oxytocin to be released, which may lessen the possibility of a toxic workplace atmosphere. The function of oxytocin is further investigated, emphasizing its ability to combat the symptoms of withdrawal in addicts and avoid physical dependency.

The chapter ends by highlighting the significant influence that relationships based on trust and love have on people's well-being. Empirical evidence bolsters the notion that intimate, trustworthy relationships are linked to increased longevity and improved well-being.

The author claims that a Circle of Safety only works when it is founded on sincere human ties, emphasizing the role oxytocin plays in forging strong bonds of trust.

In conclusion, Chapter 25 promotes the adoption of the AA program's Step 12 principles, encouraging service, sincere relationships, and the release of oxytocin as necessary elements in overcoming social obstacles and creating a better, more encouraging environment.

KEY LESSONS

NOTE DOWN THE MOST IMPORTANT LESSONS YOU LEARNED FROM THIS CHAPTER

How has your well-being at work been impacted by an emphasis on performance and numbers?

Do you feel supported and trusted by your coworkers in your present workplace? What part can you play in creating a more positive work environment?

Consider whether any elements of your company's culture or leadership style inadvertently encourage a "dopamine addiction" in your staff. How can you prioritize your team's overall well-being by addressing this?

Consider how love and trust have impacted your work experiences. What effects have these variables had on your job satisfaction and output?

SUMMARY OF CHAPTER 26

Chapter 26 addresses the problems associated with plenty in industrialized cultures, where a plentiful supply of resources encourages wasteful conduct. According to the author, less adversity causes civilizations to collaborate less, which lowers oxytocin levels—a hormone that increases the perceived worth of resources.

The author also disputes the idea that days with few problems are the most remembered, contending that days on which people work together to overcome obstacles tend to evoke more positive emotions in individuals. This togetherness causes oxytocin to be released, which strengthens interpersonal ties.

To spur creativity and dedication, the chapter highlights the need to redefine difficulty in the contemporary era of plenty and exhorts leaders to formulate problems that exceed the resources at their disposal.

The chapter ends by highlighting how crucial it is for leaders to provide a goal that exceeds resources but not intelligence, posing a challenge that motivates others to give their all.

The need for a higher purpose and purpose in directing decision-making is emphasized by providing instances of leaders who put the needs of their people ahead of their short-term financial gain.

KEY LESSONS

NOTE DOWN THE MOST IMPORTANT LESSONS YOU LEARNED FROM THIS CHAPTER

In contemporary communities, how does the availability of resources impact our understanding of their worth?

Consider your finest work-related days. Were these moments when everything went as planned or when the group overcame obstacles as a unit? How was your experience affected by common struggles?

In what way is the idea of struggle presented at work? Is it seen as a personal load or as a problem that everyone must share? What effects does this viewpoint have on creativity and teamwork?

Consider the leaders that were named, such as Steve Jobs and Bill Gates. How did their success stem from their sense of purpose? How can you use these realizations for your leadership or work?

The author tells the inspirational tale of Johnny Bravo, an A-10 pilot who discovers the value of empathy and the accountability that comes with being a leader. Being a leader is hard; it takes time, effort, and commitment to others. But as notable leaders like Charlie Kim, Bob Chapman, James Sinegal, and Captain David Marquet have shown, there are real advantages to leadership that put people first.

The chapter compares and contrasts several leadership philosophies, stressing the consistency of a methodical approach against the exhilarating qualities of a riskier tactic. According to the author, leaders need to place a high priority on establishing a robust "Circle of Safety," much like a parent who is dedicated to the welfare of their child.

The author emphasizes that change does not have to be abrupt or immediate when introducing the concept that force is equal to mass times acceleration. The transformation has been accomplished by leaders such as Bob Chapman through incremental improvements, experimentation, and letting momentum develop gradually.

Regardless of official position, everyone is encouraged

to accept leadership responsibilities in the book's concluding message. The author exhorts readers to strengthen the "Circle of Safety" by making little gestures for the welfare of others every day.

KEY LESSONS

NOTE DOWN THE MOST IMPORTANT LESSONS YOU LEARNED FROM THIS CHAPTER

As Johnny Bravo's discovery illustrates, how can you incorporate empathy into your leadership job on a moment-to-moment basis?

Consider the many leadership philosophies that have been discussed, including those of Jack Welch, Bob Chapman, Charlie Kim, and James Sinegal. Which is more consistent with your values, and how may you modify your style of leadership to reflect that?

Taking into account that being a leader means being dedicated to the welfare of others, how can you show those entrusted to your care even more dedication, and what kind of sacrifices are you prepared to make to help them succeed?

Taking into account the need for acceleration and gradual, little adjustments, how can you strike a balance between the need for drastic change and maintaining a Circle of Safety?

ACTION EXERCISES

- Organizational leaders should determine and convey a compelling mission statement. Motivate groups of people to work together toward this goal to create a feeling of purpose and commitment.
- Create a recognition program to honor people and groups that, through their work, embody the goals of the organization. Honor the times when the goal has made a good difference in someone else's life.
- Establish a forum where staff members may discuss their own experiences overcoming obstacles. Written testimonies, video interviews, or internal occurrences can all be used to accomplish this.
- Create a mentoring program in which seasoned staff members assist new hires in overcoming obstacles. Promote an environment of cooperation and shared knowledge.
- Put in place leadership development initiatives for staff members at different levels. Prioritize developing emotional intelligence, leadership abilities, and a feeling of responsibility for the welfare of others.
- Motivate staff members to identify and guide up-and-coming leaders in the company. Encourage an environment that recognizes and supports leadership at all levels.

Leadership Reflection Journal

DATE: __/__/___
S M T W TH F S

Reflection on Leadership Practices

VALUES AND ARES OF IMPROVEMENT

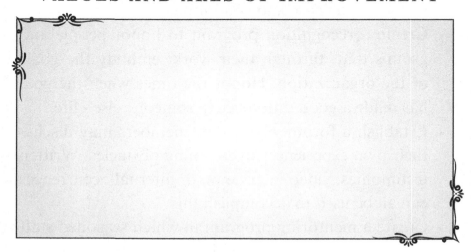

Impactful Moments

POSITIVE LEADERSHIP MOMENT AND LESSONS LEARNED

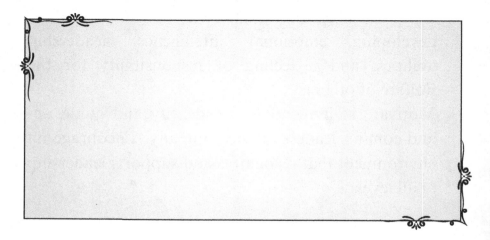

Personal Development

NEW LEADERSHIP SKILLS OR KNOWLEDGE ACQUIRED

PROGRESS TOWARDS LONG-TERM LEADERSHIP GOALS

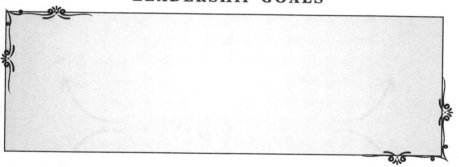

Future Action

----

6 Insights From This Section

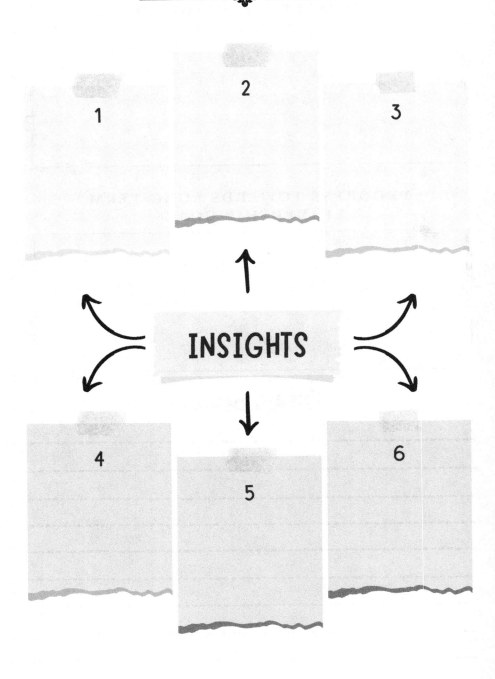

Leadership
Vision Board

VISION 1

VISION 2

VISION 3

FINAL NOTE

Congratulations on finishing your Leadership Reflection Workbook. As you get to the end of this transforming journey of self-discovery and development, remember to applaud your dedication to becoming a better leader.

Reflecting on your everyday experiences, celebrating accomplishments, and learning from obstacles are all important aspects of the ongoing road of leadership growth. Remember that leadership is a constantly evolving process, and your willingness to reflect demonstrates your passion for greatness.

As you progress, keep the lessons from this workbook in mind. Use the information collected to guide your actions, improve your approach, and create positive change in your team and company.

Leadership is a process that requires ongoing learning, flexibility, and a genuine desire to make a good difference. Your commitment to invest in your personal development puts you on track to not just lead, but lead with purpose and sincerity.

The obstacles you confront and the victories you enjoy all add to your distinctive leadership story. Accept each event as a chance to improve your talents, strengthen your relationships, and leave an indelible impression on the peo ple you lead.

Thank you for devoting time and attention to this reflection process. Your dedication to self-improvement helps not just you, but also your team and business, fostering a healthy and inspiring work culture.

As you go forward, use the lessons gained and objectives established in these pages to guide you toward further success and satisfaction. Your leadership path is continuous, with the best yet to come.

I wish you confidence, resilience, and extraordinary success in all of your leadership pursuits!

I admire your path.

KARL LUCAS

MY
NOTES

S M T W T F S

MY
NOTES

DATE:

S M T W T F S

MY
NOTES

MY
NOTES

S M T W T F S

MY
NOTES

S   M   T   W   T   F   S

MY
NOTES

DATE:

S M T W T F S

MY
NOTES

S M T W T F S

MY
NOTES

MY
NOTES

S   M   T   W   T   F   S

WORKBOOK

FOR

LEADERS
EAT LAST

*A Self Reflective Practical Guide To
Simon Sinek's Book*

Why Some Teams Pull Together
and Others Don't

Made in United States
Orlando, FL
20 September 2024

51758843R10095